OUR CHANGING EARTH

ICE AGES

Jason D. Nemeth

PowerKiDS press™

New York

Published in 2012 by The Rosen Publishing Group, Inc.
29 East 21st Street, New York, NY 10010

First Edition

Editor: Amelie von Zumbusch
Book Design: Greg Tucker

Photo Credits: Cover, pp. 4, 5, 6–7, 8, 9, 12, 16, 17 (bottom), 18, 19, 20, 21 Shutterstock.com; p. 10 Albert Moldvay/National Geographic/Getty Images; p. 11 Robyn Beck/AFP/Getty Images; p. 13 (right) Ria Novosti/AFP/Getty Images; p. 13 (left) © www.iStockphoto.com/Jakub Niezabitowski; p. 14 (main) Jerome Chatin/Gamma-Rapho via Getty Images; pp. 14–15 Jack Unruh/National Geographic/Getty Images; p. 17 (top) DEA Picture Library/Getty Images; p. 22 Hemera/Thinkstock.

Library of Congress Cataloging-in-Publication Data

Nemeth, Jason D.
 Ice ages / by Jason D. Nemeth. — 1st ed.
    p. cm. — (Our changing earth)
 Includes index.
 ISBN 978-1-4488-6167-5 (library binding) — ISBN 978-1-4488-6292-4 (pbk.) — ISBN 978-1-4488-6293-1 (6-pack)
 1. Glacial epoch—Juvenile literature. I. Title.
 QE697.N46 2012
 551.31—dc23
                              2011022773

Manufactured in the United States of America

CPSIA Compliance Information: Batch #WW12PK: For Further Information contact Rosen Publishing, New York, New York at 1-800-237-9932

CONTENTS

SNOWBALL EARTH

An ice age is a time when Earth is quite cold. The cold allows **glaciers** to form. Glaciers are large sheets of ice that grow and move. They often form on high mountains. Glaciers also build up on land near Earth's **North Pole** and **South Pole**. These are the points on Earth that are the farthest north and the farthest south.

California's Yosemite Valley was shaped during an ice age. Glaciers filled the valley at least three different times.

Today there are more than 150,000 glaciers on Earth. This is the Khumbu Glacier. It is in the Himalayas.

Ice ages can last for thousands of years. During a very cold ice age, glaciers cover most of Earth's land. About 2 billion years ago, Earth went through an ice age that was so cold that the planet was like one big snowball.

Glaciers start as snow. If it is cold enough, not all the snow melts after it falls. It stays on the ground until the next snowfall. New snow piles up on top of old snow. The snow on the bottom of the pile gets pressed down. This turns it into ice. As the snow keeps piling up, the ice does, too.

Ice weighs a lot! Glaciers grow so heavy that they slide down mountains and across the earth. Sometimes water builds up at the very bottom of a glacier. The water underneath a glacier can help it slide even faster.

The Puerto Moreno Glacier is part of the Southern Patagonian Ice Field. This is the remains of an ice sheet that covered southern South America about 18,000 years ago.

7

COMING AND GOING

Earth's ice ages come in **cycles**, or repeating patterns. Ice ages come and go over millions of years, just as summer and winter come and go over one year.

The earliest ice age that scientists know about happened over 2 billion years ago. The latest ice age started 2.5 million years ago. We are still in it today!

Many rocks on the island of Barbados are made of the remains of tiny animals called coral that lived in the Eemian period. This was the last warm period before the current one.

During an ice age, glaciers grow, melt, and grow again. When they grow, it is called a **glaciation**. When they melt, it is called an **interglacial**. The cycle of growing and melting happens about every 100,000 years. Interglacials last for around 10,000 years. We live during an interglacial today.

This boy is visiting Yellowstone National Park. About 25,000 years ago, glaciers covered most of the land that is now the park.

Scientists in the 1800s realized that glaciers move rocks from one place to another. However, rocks that looked like they had been moved by glaciers were found in many places. The scientists guessed glaciers must have once covered much of Earth.

Today, scientists study ice ages in many ways. They dig up samples of the ocean's bottom called ocean cores. Ocean cores have **fossils**,

This scientist is gathering ice cores from a glacier in the South Pole. Scientists have learned a lot about Earth's history by studying ice cores.

or the remains of dead plants and animals, in them. The fossils show whether the ocean was warm or cold when they were buried.

Ice drilled from deep within glaciers has air bubbles. The bubbles also show scientists whether Earth was hot or cold when they formed.

People also learn about ice ages from fossils buried in rocks. These people are cleaning a Columbian mammoth fossil that was found in California. These animals lived during the last glaciation.

THIS IS ZED'S PELVIS!

THE ICE AGE

The most recent time glaciers advanced is often just called the Ice Age. It started 100,000 years ago. By 20,000 years ago, glaciers covered much of Earth. They reached far into North America and Europe. Where the city of Chicago, Illinois, sits today, there was a 2-mile- (3 km) thick sheet of ice. In Europe, glaciers covered Finland, Norway, and England.

The ice sheets that covered northern North America during the Ice Age were the Greenland ice sheet, the Laurentide ice sheet, and the Cordilleran ice sheet. The Greenland ice sheet, seen here, still exists today.

Saber-toothed tigers, woolly mammoths, woolly rhinos, and giant sloths all lived during the Ice Age. These large mammals are no longer alive today. Scientists believe that they became **extinct**, or died out, because Earth warmed up and people hunted them for food.

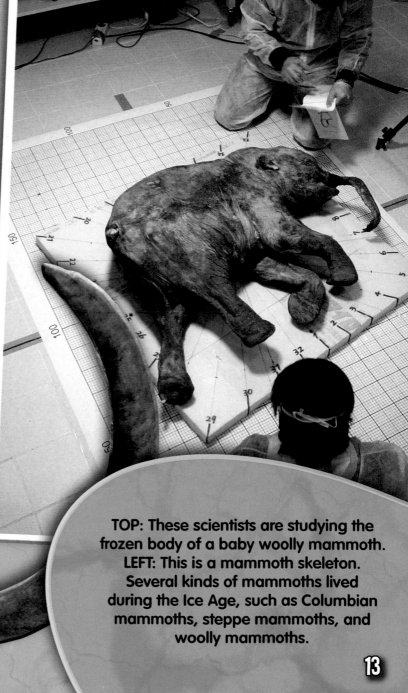

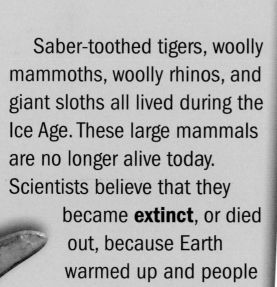

TOP: These scientists are studying the frozen body of a baby woolly mammoth. LEFT: This is a mammoth skeleton. Several kinds of mammoths lived during the Ice Age, such as Columbian mammoths, steppe mammoths, and woolly mammoths.

PEOPLE AND THE ICE AGE

The first people lived in Africa. During the Ice Age, people spread out all over the world. Africa was warm, but many other places were cold or covered in glaciers. People survived by learning new skills and making new tools.

During the Ice Age, people made these paintings of animals in a cave in what is now Lascaux, France.

Scientists have found the remains of houses that people built out of mammoth bones during the Ice Age. This picture shows what these houses might have looked like.

People used spears and axes to hunt woolly mammoths and other animals for food. They used needles to sew animal skins into clothing to keep warm. People used fire to cook and stay warm.

During the Ice Age, people followed food sources, such as animal herds, around. People sometimes also moved to find warmer homes.

ICE CHANGES THE WORLD

The Ice Age shaped the world in many ways. It allowed people who lived in Asia to come to North America for the first time. There was so much water frozen in glaciers that the oceans were much lower than they are today. People could walk from Siberia to Alaska on dry land.

Acadia National Park, in Maine, was shaped by glaciers during the Ice Age. In fact, glaciers helped shape all of New England and the Upper Midwest.

The Ice Age also shaped land. Glaciers cut deep valleys in some places and left high piles of rock in other places. Many of these can still be seen today. Moving glaciers shaped the Great Lakes. The lakes were filled with water as the glaciers melted.

TOP: This picture shows people walking from Asia to North America during the Ice Age. The land they walked across is now covered in water and known as the Bering Strait. BOTTOM: Lake Michigan is one of the Great Lakes.

Scientists are still learning how ice ages work. They discovered that glaciers need land to form. They usually start growing at Earth's poles. Sometimes the poles are covered in oceans instead of land. This happens because the **plates** that make up Earth's outside move very slowly. When there is no land at the poles, an ice age cannot happen.

Earth gets most of its warmth from the Sun. This is why changes in the amount of the Sun's heat that reaches Earth make it hotter or colder.

Also, Earth travels around the Sun. Its path around the Sun is Earth's **orbit**. Sometimes Earth's orbit brings it closer to the Sun. Other times it gets farther away. When it gets far away, Earth grows cold enough for an ice age to start.

Earth's axis is the imaginary line around which it spins. Changes in the axis's angle may help start ice ages.

← Axis

GREENHOUSE GASES

When Earth is cold and there is land at the poles, an ice age still might not happen. There also must be few **greenhouse gases** in the **atmosphere**. The atmosphere is the layers of air around Earth. Greenhouse gases, such as

People and other animals have bodies that make carbon dioxide. When we breathe, we let out carbon dioxide.

carbon dioxide, trap the Sun's heat. This warms Earth. Too many greenhouse gases will make Earth too warm for an ice age to start.

When there are few greenhouse gases, heat from the Sun escapes Earth. This makes it colder. Past ice ages may have happened because Earth's plants sucked much of the carbon dioxide out of the air.

Plants take in carbon dioxide. They use it to make sugars. These sugars are the way they store the energy they need to live and grow.

THE NEXT ICE AGE

If the cycle continues, scientists think it will reach its coldest point in 80,000 years. They are not sure when glaciers will start to advance, though. They are unsure because people are adding many greenhouse gases to the air by burning oil and coal for fuel. This might keep Earth warmer for longer.

We cannot be sure when glaciers will start to advance, but we know it will happen. Millions of years of Earth history tell us that it will someday get colder.

Today, glaciers cover less land than they did during the past. There are still many places we can see these huge sheets of ice, though.

GLOSSARY

atmosphere (AT-muh-sfeer) The gases around an object in space. On Earth this is air.

carbon dioxide (KAHR-bun dy-OK-syd) A gas with no smell or color. People breathe out carbon dioxide.

cycles (SY-kulz) Actions that happen in the same order over and over.

extinct (ik-STINGKT) No longer existing.

fossils (FO-sulz) The hardened remains of dead animals or plants.

glaciation (glay-shee-AY-shun) The time during an ice age in which it is coldest and glaciers grow.

glaciers (GLAY-shurz) Large masses of ice that move down mountains or along valleys.

greenhouse gases (GREEN-hows GAS-ez) Gases that trap heat near Earth when they are in Earth's atmosphere.

interglacial (in-ter-GLAY-shul) The time during an ice age in which it gets warmer.

North Pole (NORTH POHL) The northernmost point on Earth.

orbit (OR-bit) A circular path.

plates (PLAYTS) The moving pieces of Earth's crust, the top layer of Earth.

South Pole (SOWTH POHL) The southernmost point on Earth.

INDEX

WEB SITES

Due to the changing nature of Internet links, PowerKids Press has developed an online list of Web sites related to the subject of this book. This site is updated regularly. Please use this link to access the list:
www.powerkidslinks.com/chng/ice/